Tennant/Tennent

by Iain Gray

Lang**Syne**

PUBLISHING

WRITING *to* REMEMBER

79 Main Street, Newtongrange,
Midlothian EH22 4NA
Tel: 0131 344 0414   Fax: 0845 075 6085
E-mail: info@lang-syne.co.uk
www.langsyneshop.co.uk

Design by Dorothy Meikle
Printed by Printwell Ltd
© Lang Syne Publishers Ltd 2022

All rights reserved. No part of this publication may be reproduced, stored or introduced into a retrieval system, or transmitted in any form or by any means (electronic, mechanical, photocopying, recording or otherwise) without the prior written permission of Lang Syne Publishers Ltd.

ISBN 978-1-85217-794-2

Tennant/Tennent

MOTTO:
God will fill our sails

CREST:
A ship's sail

TERRITORY:
West Lothian

NAME variations include:
- Tenman
- Tenand
- Tennan
- Tennand
- Tennend

Chapter one:

The origins of popular surnames

by George Forbes and Iain Gray

If you don't know where you came from, you won't know where you're going **is a frequently quoted observation and one that has a particular resonance today when there has been a marked upsurge in interest in genealogy, with increasing numbers of people curious to trace their family roots.**

Main sources for genealogical research include census returns and official records of births, marriages and deaths – and the key to unlocking the detail they contain is obviously a family surname, one that has been 'inherited' and passed from generation to generation.

No matter our station in life, we all have a surname – but it was not until about the middle of the fourteenth century that the practice of being identified by a particular surname became commonly established throughout the British Isles.

Previous to this, it was normal for a person to be identified through the use of only a forename.

But as population gradually increased and there were many more people with the same forename, surnames were adopted to distinguish one person, or community, from another.

Many common English surnames are patronymic in origin, meaning they stem from the forename of one's father – with 'Johnson,' for example, indicating 'son of John.'

It was the Normans, in the wake of their eleventh century conquest of Anglo-Saxon England, a pivotal moment in the nation's history, who first brought surnames into usage – although it was a gradual process.

For the Normans, these were names initially based on the title of their estates, local villages and chateaux in France to distinguish and identify these landholdings.

Such grand descriptions also helped enhance the prestige of these warlords and generally glorify their lofty positions high above the humble serfs slaving away below in the pecking order who had only single names, often with Biblical connotations as in Pierre and Jacques.

The only descriptive distinctions among the peasantry concerned their occupations, like 'Pierre the swineherd' or 'Jacques the ferryman.'

Roots of surnames that came into usage in England not only included Norman-French, but also Old French, Old Norse, Old English, Middle English, German, Latin, Greek, Hebrew and the Gaelic languages of the Celts.

The Normans themselves were originally Vikings, or 'Northmen', who raided, colonised and eventually settled down around the French coastline.

They had sailed up the Seine in their long-boats in 900AD under their ferocious leader Rollo and ruled the roost in north eastern France before sailing over to conquer England in 1066 under Duke William of Normandy – better known to posterity as William the Conqueror, or King William I of England.

Granted lands in the newly-conquered England, some of their descendants later acquired territories in Wales, Scotland and Ireland – taking not only their own surnames, but also the practice of adopting a surname, with them.

But it was in England where Norman rule and custom first impacted, particularly in relation to the adoption of surnames.

This is reflected in the famous *Domesday Book*, a massive survey of much of England and Wales, ordered by William I, to determine who owned what, what it was worth and therefore how much they were liable to pay in taxes to the voracious Royal Exchequer.

Completed in 1086 and now held in the National Archives in Kew, London, 'Domesday' was an Old English word meaning 'Day of Judgement.'

This was because, in the words of one contemporary chronicler, "its decisions, like those of the Last Judgement, are unalterable."

It had been a requirement of all those English landholders – from the richest to the poorest – that they identify themselves for the purposes of the survey and for future reference by means of a surname.

This is why the *Domesday Book*, although written in Latin as was the practice for several centuries with both civic and ecclesiastical records, is an invaluable source for the early appearance of a wide range of English surnames.

Several of these names were coined in connection with occupations.

These include Baker and Smith, while Cooks, Chamberlains, Constables and Porters were to be found carrying out duties in large medieval households.

The church's influence can be found in names such as Bishop, Friar and Monk while the popular name of Bennett derives from the late fifth to mid-sixth century Saint Benedict, founder of the Benedictine order of monks.

The early medical profession is represented by Barber, while businessmen produced names that include Merchant and Sellers.

Down at the village watermill, the names that cropped up included Millar/Miller, Walker and Fuller, while other self-explanatory trades included Cooper, Tailor, Mason and Wright.

Even the scenery was utilised as in Moor, Hill, Wood and Forrest – while the hunt and the chase supplied names that include Hunter, Falconer, Fowler and Fox.

Colours are also a source of popular surnames, as in Black, Brown, Gray/Grey, Green and White, and would have denoted the colour of the clothing the person habitually wore or, apart from the obvious exception of 'Green', one's hair colouring or even complexion.

The surname Red developed into Reid, while

Blue was rare and no-one wanted to be associated with yellow.

Rather self-important individuals took surnames that include Goodman and Wiseman, while physical attributes crept into surnames such as Small and Little.

Many families proudly boast the heraldic device known as a Coat of Arms, as featured on our front cover.

The central motif of the Coat of Arms would originally have been what was sometimes borne on the shield of a warrior to distinguish himself from others on the battlefield.

Not featured on the Coat of Arms, but highlighted on page three, are the family motto and related crest – with the latter frequently different from the central motif.

Adding further variety to the rich cultural heritage that is represented by surnames is the appearance in recent times in lists of the most common names found throughout the United Kingdom of ones that include Khan, Patel and Singh – names that have proud roots in the vast sub-continent of India.

Echoes of a far distant past can still be found in our surnames and they can be borne with pride in commemoration of our forebears.

Chapter two:

By royal command

Derived from the Old French 'tenant', in turn stemming from 'tenir', meaning 'to hold', 'Tennant' and its popular spelling variant 'Tennent' originally denoted a tenant farmer – someone who 'held' land from an overlord to whom he in return payed a rent either in the form of cash or produce.

Found throughout the British Isles, in Scotland it came to be particularly identified with the former county of Linlithgowshire, now West Lothian, and where from approximately 1150 a family of the name was established at a location known as Creston, or Crestone.

In the now redundant form 'Tenaunt', a Thomas Tenaunt is recorded in Edinburgh in 1309 while, in the form 'Tennand', a John Tennand appears in 1366 as a merchant and civic official in Stirling.

Slightly further down the social scale, in the form 'Tenant', a John Tenant appears in a military capacity as a member of the garrison at Edinburgh Castle in 1339.

Engaged in more important duties in the

royal residence, however, John Tennent was the particularly colourful character who was not only a servant to King James V but also one of his close friends and confidants – the pair at one point colluding in a bizarre stunt concerning a prospective bride for the monarch.

Tennent's date of birth is not known, but he appears to have been a member of the gentry with his own property, Listonshiels, in the parish of Kirkliston, west of Edinburgh.

As purse-master to the king, he was responsible, quite literally, for carrying his cash as he travelled on his frequent trips throughout the kingdom, dispensing alms to the needy.

In addition to his role of purse-master, Tennant was also master of the royal wardrobe, overseeing the duties of a small army of not only tailors and embroiderers but also a laundry.

As if these onerous duties were not enough, he was also entrusted with the safe-keeping of the sacred and precious Honours of Scotland of Sceptre, Crown and Sword – and is recorded as ordering a new case for the latter in 1539.

Three years earlier, in 1536, the pressure had been on the 24-year-old James to find a suitable bride.

A previous project for his marriage to Princess Mary, daughter of King Henry VIII, had been all but abandoned, as was a plan for his marriage to Mary of Portugal.

It was finally arranged through a tortuously worked out treaty that he should marry Marie of Bourbon, a daughter of the French Duke of Vendome.

James had the reputation of having an eye for a pretty woman and was less than impressed with the physical attributes of his bride-to-be when shown her portrait.

He was so dismayed that he demanded that in addition to the dowry of 100,000 livres that had been agreed, he should receive a pension of 20,000 livres – the then currency of France roughly equivalent to one pound in Scottish currency.

Ever impetuous and headstrong, James intended setting off for France as a private wanderer, accompanied by only a small retinue including his faithful servant and companion John Tennent.

But a combination of fear of capture by an English vessel and contrary winds meant that after leaving Leith his vessel drifted around Scotland until he found himself in the Firth of Clyde.

Wiser heads eventually prevailed, and James

and his entourage of courtly hangers-on, plus 500 soldiers and, of course, Tennent, embarked from Pittenweem in a fleet of seven vessels on September 1, 1536.

Reaching Dieppe, they travelled overland to Paris where James was to meet Marie of Bourbon.

James had been in the habit of travelling among his Scottish subjects in the 'incognito' persona of 'the Gudeman of Ballengeich', but he added a twist to this before the meeting – for reasons best known to himself – by instructing Tennent to swap clothes with him.

It is not known if the hapless Marie saw through the disguise and what her reaction was – but what is known is that, at least in James's eyes, her portrait appears to have not been quite accurate.

In the flesh, he found her even more physically unappealing, but all was not lost, as his roving eye alighted on the charms of the Princess Magdalen – or Madeleine – a daughter of King Francis I.

Born on August 10, 1520 at Chateau St Germain-en-Laye, the 16-year-old Madeleine of Valois possessed a haunting and fragile beauty.

This rather timid daughter of the French

court appears to have been genuinely enamoured by her extrovert Scottish admirer and, despite warnings that her frail constitution would not be able to cope with the harsh Scottish climate, the couple were married at Notre Dame, Paris, on January 1, 1537.

This was accompanied with great pomp and ceremony, with James suitably and magnificently attired thanks to Tennent.

Meanwhile the king and his entourage caused quite a stir when in Paris.

His fellow countrymen, rather in the manner of a present-day Tartan Army of travelling football supporters, enjoyed to the full all the sophisticated delights the French court had to offer – the hospitality, of course, being free.

Acting like any tourist in Paris, James went on shopping trips, accompanied by his purse-bearer John Tennent.

Madeleine, the new Scottish queen, took ill about three months after the marriage, but recovered sufficiently for the newly-weds to set sail for Scotland and disembark at Leith on May 28, 1537.

Tragically, she had less than six weeks to enjoy her new role of Queen of Scots – dying in

Holyrood Palace, probably from tuberculosis, on July 7.

She was only a few weeks short of her seventeenth birthday and, because of her brief reign, has become known to posterity as 'the Summer Queen'.

Buried in the rather dry official documents of the time we find that her funeral involved, for the first time in Scotland, the wearing of black as a symbol of mourning.

Ordered by John Tennent in his capacity of master of the wardrobe, the royal treasurer's accounts detail payments for a black saddlecloth for the king and an ell of 'Paris black' for his shoes.

The gowns for the dead queen's French ladies-in-waiting were 'made in the fashion of priests' gowns, white satin to be crosses upon the black velvet.'

Thirty ells of 'Holland cloth' made up the veils of these French ladies, while for the queen's nine pages and three other servants, 'black doublets, hose and bonnets, Scotch black, French black, and Paris black' were provided.

Dynastic considerations meant James had little time to mourn.

Less than one year later, in June of 1538, his

marriage to Mary of Guise, daughter of the Duke of Guise and future mother of the ill-fated Mary Queen of Scots, was celebrated at St Andrews.

James died in 1542 following the Scottish defeat at the battle of Solway Moss and, by custom, John Tennent was charged with distributing his wardrobe among favourites.

The king's former and faithful servant, who had married Mavis Acheson, a royal laundress, died seven years later, with his estate passing to his brother Patrick Tennent.

Also in the sixteenth century, but in the west of Scotland and again with the popular Tennant spelling variant 'Tennent', Robert Tennent laid the foundations for what became the family brewing business J. and R. Tennent.

Little is known of him beyond the fact that the small enterprise he set up on the banks of the Molendinar Burn in the east end of Glasgow became, in the 1760s and through his descendant Hugh Tennent, Tennent's Well Park Brewery.

Under Hugh Tennent, born in 1863 and who died in 1890, the business vastly expanded after he visited Bavaria to study German brewing techniques.

Originally manufacturing strong export ales

and stout, the company produced its first Tennent's Lager in 1885 – later famous worldwide for not only its taste but also the design of its cans featuring photographs of Scottish models known as the 'Lager Lovelies'.

Having undergone a number of changes in ownership and mergers over the years, the company is now part of the C&C Group (Cantrell and Cochrane), while in the past it has also sponsored a range of events including, from 1994 to 2016, the T in the Park outdoor music festival.

Chapter three:

Bright Young Things

Travelling forwards in time from the sixteenth to the late eighteenth and early nineteenth centuries, Charles Tennant was the Scottish weaver, chemist and industrialist who established a noted family dynasty that has included a colourful cast of characters including politicians, peers, philanthropists, socialites and eccentrics.

Born in 1768 at Laigh Corton, near Alloway, Ayrshire, the son of a farmer, when a young lad the family moved to nearby Glenconner, Ochiltree, and he was later apprenticed to the highly skilled trade of handloom weaving.

Immersing himself in all aspects of what was then Scotland's main industry, he realised a major restriction to production was the time-consuming method used to bleach cloth before it could be woven.

In a primitive practice dating back centuries, cloth was steeped in stale urine and then exposed to sunlight in 'bleach fields' for a number of months before considered satisfactorily treated.

In some cases this could take up to eighteen

months, severely holding up production and, in a bid to resolve this, in 1788 Tennant bought bleaching fields at Darnley, near Barrhead, Renfrewshire.

Training himself in chemical processes, he experimented for a number of years with a mixture of lime and chlorine and, in 1794, formed a partnership with three others including the chemist Charles Macintosh, famed as the inventor of waterproofing.

With the help of Macintosh, Tennant developed a bleaching powder and registered its first patent in 1799.

Formed through a process of reacting chlorine with dry slaked lime, the powder proved an instant success and Tennant built a chemical works at St Rollox, in the north of Glasgow, to produce vast quantities for sale throughout the world.

Employing more than 1,000 people at one stage and, throughout the 1830s and 1840s, the largest chemical works in the world – covering 100 acres – its 435.5ft (132.7m) high chimney, known as the St Rollox Stalk or Tennant's Stalk, was a well-known landmark until it had to be demolished in 1922 after being struck by lightning.

Originally known as Charles Tennant and Company, the business burgeoned to the manufacture of explosives, while the chemical side of the enterprise later became known as the United Alkali Company Ltd., merging with other companies in 1926 to form Imperial Chemical Industries (ICI).

Also noted as an advocate of social reform, Charles Tennant died in 1838.

Through his son John Tennant he was the grandfather of the Scottish Liberal Party politician and industrialist Charles Clow Tennant, later more formally known as Sir Charles Clow Tennant, 1st Baronet.

Born in 1823, he carried on the family business in addition to establishing C. Tennant Sons and Company as a merchant bank in the City of London.

Serving from 1879 to 1880 as Member of Parliament (MP) for Glasgow and, from 1880 to 1886 for Peebles and Selkirk, he was created a Baronet in 1852 – the same year he purchased the 3,500 acre estate The Glen, located in the glen of the Quair Water, south east of Peebles and near Innerleithen, in the Scottish Borders.

Glen House, which he commissioned the architect David Bryce to rebuild in Scottish Baronial style, is now a Category A Listed Building, while the grounds are included in the Inventory of Gardens and Designed Landscapes in Scotland.

Still in the possession of the family, it is used as a conference venue and also features as a film location.

Married from 1849 until her death in 1895 to Emma Winsloe, Sir Charles Tennant's second wife was the talented amateur musician Margaret Miles, a cousin of the banker and politician Sir Philip Miles.

One of his gifts to her was what is now known as the Lady Tennant Stradivarius, a violin made by Antonio Stradivari of Cremona in 1699; sold by the Tennants in 1925 and subsequently passing through a number of owners, it went for $2,032,000 at auction by Christies, New York, in 2005.

Sir Charles died in 1906, while through his first marriage he was the father of the socialite and author Margo Tennant, born in 1864 and who, following her marriage to H.H. Asquith who served as British Prime Minister from 1864 until 1928, was known as Emma Margaret Asquith, Countess of Oxford and Asquith; she died in 1945.

One of her brothers was the Liberal Party politician, industrialist and philanthropist Sir Edward Priaulx Tennant, 2nd Baronet and 1st Baron Glenconner.

Born in 1859 and succeeding his father in the family business, he served as MP for the English constituency Salisbury from 1906 to 1910, while posts he held outside politics included Lord High Commissioner for the General Assembly of the Church of Scotland, president of the Scottish Modern Arts Association and of the Edinburgh Sir Walter Scott Club.

Dryburgh Abbey, in the Borders, is where the great antiquarian and novelist Sir Walter is buried and, having bought it in 1918, Baron Glenconner gifted the abbey to the nation to save it from ruin – while also donating large sums of money to a number of other heritage initiatives and charitable causes.

Having been raised to the peerage in 1911 as Baron Glenconner, of The Glen, in the County of Peebles, he died in 1920, while he was the first husband of the author Pamela Wyndham, born in 1871 and who after his death married Edward Grey, 1st Viscount Grey of Fallodon.

She died in 1928, while one of her three sons through her first marriage was the war poet Lt. Edward Wyndham Tennant, born in 1897 and who was killed at the battle of the Somme in 1916.

Her two younger sons were the aristocrats

and socialites Stephen Tennant and David Pax Tennant.

Born in 1906, Stephen Tennant became celebrated throughout the 1920s and 30s as 'The Brightest', of the privileged social set The Bright Young Things – and one of the inspirations for the character Lord Sebastian Flyte in Evelyn Waugh's novel *Brideshead Revisited* and the model for Cedric Hampton in Nancy Mitford's *Love in a Cold Climate*.

A lover of the poet Siegfried Sassoon, he is also reputed to have proposed marriage to a friend, Elizabeth Lowndes – but she understandably turned him down after he discussed plans with her to bring his nanny along on the honeymoon.

He died in 1987, while an archive of his fascinating correspondence, artworks and ephemera is held by the Viktor Wynd Museum of Curiosities, Fine Art and Natural History, in Hackney, London.

Also a celebrated Bright Young Thing, his brother David Pax Tennant, born in 1902, was the founder when aged 23 of the bohemian private members' club The Gargoyle, in London's Soho district.

A place where aristocrats drank and rubbed shoulders with an eccentric mix of writers and artists including Lucien Freud, it remained in his possession until sold in 1952.

Renowned for hosting lavish events including 'pyjamas-and-bottles parties', where guests arrived dressed in outlandish night attire clutching bottles of alcohol, rather ironically he was also employed for a time in the decidedly staid and respectable role of an announcer for the BBC.

Married for a time to the actress Hermione Baddeley and then to Virginia Parsons, a granddaughter of the distinguished actor and manager Sir Herbert Beerbohm Tree, followed by Shelagh Rainey, sister of the fashion designer Michael Rainey, he died in 1968.

Born in 1926, Colin Tennant, 3rd Baron Glenconner, was the socialite whose wife Lady Anne Tennant (née Coke) was a lady-in-waiting to Princess Margaret.

Known for his extravagant lifestyle, he bought the Caribbean island Mustique in 1958, transforming it into an exclusive haven for jet-setting friends and acquaintances including the princess.

He died in 2010, while he is portrayed by the actor Pip Carter in the Netflix television series *The Crown*.

Chapter four:

On the world stage

From music and the stage to sport and art, bearers of the Tennant name have gained fame and acclaim.

In the world of music, **Neil Tennant** is the English singer, songwriter and former journalist who co-founded the synth-pop duo Pet Shop Boys.

Born in 1954 in North Shields, near Newcastle upon Tyne, after graduating with a degree in history he worked as London editor for Marvel UK, responsible for anglicising content of *Marvel Comics* to suit British readers.

Later working for a number of other publications, he was appointed assistant editor of the pop magazine *Smash Hits* in 1982, in the course of which he met record producer Bobby Orlando.

Having just formed Pet Shop Boys with Chris Lowe, Tennant had told the producer how they had already written some songs – and Orlando went on to produce their first hit single, the 1984 *West End Girls*.

Further hit singles have followed, including *It's a Sin*, *Always on My Mind*, *Heart* and, in a duet with Dusty Springfield, *What Have I Done to Deserve This?*

With more than 100 million record sales worldwide, the recipients of three Brit Awards and six Grammy nominations, in 2017 the duo received the NME's (New Musical Express) Godlike Genius Award.

From music to the stage and with an odd link to Neil Tennant, David John McDonald is the Scottish actor better known as **David Tennant**.

Born in 1971 in Bathgate, West Lothian but raised in Ralston, Renfrewshire, where his father Alexander "Sandy" McDonald was the local minister and who also served for a time as Moderator of the General Assembly of the Church of Scotland, his great-grandparents through his mother Helen, née McLeod, were staunch Northern Irish Protestants.

Aged only three, he informed his parents he wanted to be an actor because he was a fan – rather ironically as it turned out – of the popular television sci-fi series Doctor Who.

Despite their initial misgivings about his chosen career, they relented after being told by the Scottish actress Edith MacArthur, who saw him perform on stage when aged 11, that he had talent.

Aged 16, he became one of the youngest students to audition for the Royal Scottish Academy of Music and Drama and studied there from the age of 17 until he was 20.

The success that had been predicted nine years earlier came quickly while, after discovering that the actors' union Equity already had a 'John McDonald' on its books, he decided to take a stage name.

Reading through a copy of *Smash Hits* he came across a story on Neil Tennant of Pet Shop Boys fame, and resolved to adopt his surname.

To meet Screen Actors Guild rules, he then had to legally change his name.

First appearing on stage as a professional actor in a 7:84 Theatre Company production of *The Resistible Rise of Arturo Ui*, in 1996 he performed with the Royal Shakespeare Company (RSC) in *As You Like It*, while in 2009 he played the title role in RSC's *Hamlet*.

Major television and film credits include the 2005 *Casanova*, the same year in which he played Barty Crouch Jr. in the film *Harry Potter and the Goblet of Fire* and between 2013 and 2017 as Detective Inspector Alec Hardy in the series *Broadchurch*.

Other television credits include the 2020 *Good Omens*, with Michael Sheen, *Deadwater Fell* and, in the same year, the three-part crime drama series *Des*, in which he played the role of the Scottish serial killer Dennis Nilsen.

But one role for which he is particularly noted is playing the tenth incarnation of The Doctor in *Doctor Who*, from 2005 to 2010.

It was while filming the series in 2008 that he met his future wife, who played the role of his genetically engineered daughter.

The couple married in 2011, while his wife **Georgia Tennant** is the daughter of the actor Peter Moffett, better known by his stage name Peter Davison and who, by weird coincidence, played the fifth incarnation of The Doctor in the 1980s.

Born in London in 1984, her other television credits include *The Bill*, the drama series *Where the Heart Is* and, appearing beside her father, *The Last Detective*.

Born in London in 1950, **Victoria Tennant** is the English film and television actress whose father was the producer and talent agent Cecil Tennant and mother the Russian prima ballerina Irina Baranova.

Film credits include the 1985 *The Holcroft*

Covenant and the 1990 *The Handmaid's Tale* and, starring with Steve Martin, the 1990 *All of Me* and the 1991 *L.A. Story*, while she is also known for her role of Pamela Tudsbury in the television miniseries *The Winds of War and War* and *Remembrance*, with Robert Mitchum.

Bearers of the Tennant name have also excelled in the highly competitive world of sport.

On the cricket pitch, Andrew Tennant, better known as **Andy Tennant**, is the Scottish former player born in Ayr in 1966.

Having represented Scotland on a 1993-94 tour of Zimbabwe as a left-arm orthodox spinner and at club level for Prestwick Cricket Club, he was appointed director of Cricket Scotland in 2014.

From sport to the creative world of art, **Dorothy Tennant** was a noted English painter of the Victorian era neoclassicism school.

Born in London in 1855, her father Charles Tennant was a wealthy landowner and politician while her mother Gertrude Barbara Rich Collier was a society hostess and suffragist.

Studying painting in both London and Paris and her work featuring in a number of exhibitions including the Royal Academy in 1886, she became known as Lady Stanley following her marriage in 1890 to the African explorer Henry Morton Stanley.

Also an author and editor of her husband's autobiography – carefully removing any reference to the other women in his life – she died in 1926.

One of her sisters was the photographer **Eveleen Tennant Myers**, born in London in 1856.

Married to the paranormal researcher and classicist Frederick William Henry Myers, she posed for the Pre-Raphaelite painters John Everett Millais and George Frederic Watts before taking up photography.

She died in 1937, while the National Portrait Gallery, London, holds more than 200 of her photographic portraits.

In the world of literature, **Kathleen Kylie Tennant** was the award-winning Australian novelist, short story writer, historian, biographer and critic born in 1912 in Manly, New South Wales.

Immersing herself in the experiences of the people she wrote about, she travelled widely throughout her native land, including as an itinerant worker during the years of the nation's economic depression and even spending some time in prison for research purposes.

Both her 1941 novel *The Battlers* and the 1943 *Ride on Stranger*, set in the 1930s, have been adapted for television miniseries.

The recipient of an Australian Literature Society Gold Medal for *The Battlers* and made an Officer of the Order of Australia for services to literature, she died in 1988.

From literature to ballet, **Veronica Tennant**, born in London in 1946 but immigrating to Canada with her family as a child, became the youngest person ever, when aged 18, to enter the National Ballet of Canada.

Making her debut in the principal role in *Romeo and Juliet*, in 1976 she toured North America, Europe and Japan as principal ballerina along with other ballet greats including Rudolf Nureyev.

Made a Companion of the Order of Canada in 2003, a year later she received the Governor General's Performing Arts Award for Lifetime Artistic Achievement – the nation's highest honour in the performing arts.

On the catwalk, **Stella Tennant** was the British model born in the Scottish Borders in 1970 and whose parents were The Hon. Tobias William Tennant, son of the 2nd Baron Glenconner and Lady

Emma Cavendish, daughter of Andrew Cavendish, 11th Duke of Devonshire.

Attracting the attention of the fashion photographers Bruce Weber and Steven Meisel when aged 23 and noted for her androgynous look, she went on to enjoy great success as a model, including in campaigns for Chanel, Calvin Klein, Burberry and Hermès.

One of the British models who sported fashions by British designers for the closing ceremony of the 2012 London Olympics and an inductee of the Scottish Fashion Awards Hall of Fame, in 1999 she married the French photographer David Lasnet in her home village of Oxnam, Roxburghshire.

Having suffered from mental health problems, she took her own life in 2020, only five days after her fiftieth birthday, while it was also revealed she and her husband had quietly separated some months earlier.